Workbook
Pre-Intermediate

Smart

Da A. Hill

Contents

Unit 1	4
Unit 2	10
Unit 3	16
Unit 4	22
Unit 5	28
Stopover One	34
Unit 6	36
Unit 7	42
Unit 8	48
Unit 9	54
Unit 10	60
Stopover Two	66

Unit 1

1 **What are you doing now?**
Write five things that you are doing now.

a I'm sitting *in my bedroom at home.*
b I'm sitting ....
c I'm wearing ....
d I'm ....
e I'm ....
f I'm ....

2 **What do you usually do?**
Complete these sentences about yourself.

a At 9 a.m. on Mondays I *usually have a Maths lesson.*
b At 9 a.m. on Wednesdays I ....
c At 2 p.m. on Tuesdays I ....
d At 8 p.m. on Fridays I ....
e At 10 a.m. on Saturdays my mother ....
f At 4 p.m. on Sundays my friend ....
g At 9 p.m. on Saturdays I ....

3 **Ordering words**
Write the words in the sentences in the correct order.

a in/lives/he/my/street *He lives in my street.*
b am/homework/I/now/doing ....
c at/to/goes/o'clock/Paul/school/usually/eight ......
d brother/is/little/old/how/your/? ....
e does/doing/what/father/?/like/Paul's ....
f lot/you/computers/about/do/know/?/a ....
g in/is/Lucy/very/acting/interested ....
h hasn't/computer/home/got/Monica/a/at ....
i David's/is/at/studying/university/?/sister ....

4a Writing short answers
Write true short answers to the following questions.

a Do you live in London? *No, I don't.*
b Do you like swimming? ....
c Have you got a sister? ....
d Are you in class now? ....
e Is your mother a teacher? ....
f Does your uncle work in a bank? ....
g Do you live in a flat? ....
h Have your parents got a car? ....
i Do you collect stamps? ....
j Is it sunny today? ....
k Are you interested in tennis? ....

4b Choose five of the questions from 4a and ask them to some of your friends.
Write about their answers.

Example: You ask: *Pál, does your uncle work in a bank?*
          Pál answers: *No, he doesn't.*
          You write: *Pál's uncle doesn't work in a bank.*

....
....
....
....
....

5 Smart Moves vocabulary
Write the jumbled words correctly.

a Smart Moves is a *smafou* band.
   famous

b Jake is Pete's *nwit rrobhte*.
   ....

c Suzie is Jake and Pete's *scinou*.
   ....

d Ellen's dad is Smart Moves' *renmaag*.
   ....

e Smart Moves travel around on their *orut sub*. ....

f Smart Moves' first record was called *scatFinat*. ....

6 Guided writing
Write 100 words about a real band that you like very much. Remember to write the names of the band members, where they are from, the names of some of their songs. Finish by saying why you like the band so much.

My favourite band ....
....
....
....
....

7 Space acrostic
Answer the clues across to find out what the word down is.

a Earth is part of this system.
b Earth is one, so is Mars and Jupiter.
c You look at the stars from this place.
d You look at the stars through one of these.
e This a word for everything we can see at night.
f This is the scientist who studies e.
g A group of stars is called this.
h The star which the earth goes round.

a | S | | | | S | Y | S | T | E | M
b | | | | | L | | | T | |
c | O | B | | | | | | | |
d | | | | C | | P | E | | |
e | U | N | | | | | | | |
f | | T | R | | | E | R | | |
g | | | G | | | | | | |
h | S | | | | | | | | |

8 Articles
Put an indefinite (*a/an*) or definite (*the*) article in each space.

a Paul: Look! There's *a*......... ball in the corner of the garden.
   Liz: That's .... ball which I lost yesterday.
b John: Have you got .... pen?
   Sue: Where's .... pen I gave you for your birthday?
c Andy: Has Steve got .... old bike or .... new one?
   Mike: He's got .... old bike; it's .... one which his father gave him.
d Jane: Who's .... tall man with grey hair talking to your mother?
   Angi: He's .... man who's going to buy our house.
e Kate: What's .... platypus like?
   Dave: It's .... strange Australian animal with .... beak like a duck.

9 Correction
A student wrote about himself, but he made a lot of mistakes. Can you correct his work? Underline the mistake, and write the correct word below.

i like swimming very much, and everry day I goes to the pool. The waiter is very warm

I......swimming..

and blew, and when I go in the mornning there isn't many peoples there. I usualy swim

....

up an down the pool about twlev times, and after that I has a shower and dry myslef.

....

I often vizit the café then, and have a glass of orange jiuce before I going home.

....

10 Pronunciation
Do the words below sound the same or different? Put a tick (✓) if they are the same or a cross (✗) if they are different.

word 1	word 2	same sound or different?
busy	dizzy	...✓................
laugh	half	....
share	were	....
show	cow	....
could	good	....
waste	past	....
miss	is	....
face	space	....
move	love	....
wait	eight	....
wrong	song	....
know	now	....

11a Read this article.

Astronomy

ASTRONOMY is becoming a very popular hobby. Children everywhere are asking their parents to buy them books which show the names of the stars and planets in our universe, and also the telescopes they need to see them better.

This interest in studying the stars grew when the Hale-Bopp comet came near the Earth in 1998, then with the total eclipse of the Sun in 2000 and the total eclipse of the Moon in 2001. Everyone in Europe was able to see these things clearly.

Now young people all over the world are watching the sky to learn the names and positions of the planets and galaxies, and see how they change a little bit each night. Perhaps many of them hope that they are lucky like the amateur astronomers Mr Hale and Mr Bopp, who found the comet that has their name while looking through telescopes at home.

When some children look at the stars, they dream that one day they will be astronauts working on a space station like the Russian Mir station which came back to Earth in 2001. Others want to become space tourists like Mr Tito in 2001, and hope to visit the Moon or Mars for their holidays.

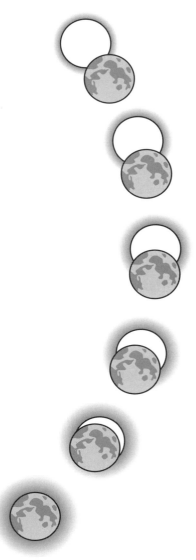

11b Answer these questions.

a Why do many children want telescopes?

....
....

b What three things made many people interested in Astronomy?

....
....

c What changes in the night sky every night?

....
....

d What did Hale and Bopp do?

....
....

e Who is Mr Tito?

....
....

12 Summary writing

Look at the article about Astronomy on p. 8 again. It has four paragraphs. When you write a short summary, you need to note the main information in each paragraph, then put it together to make one sentence. Here is the main information from the Astronomy article:

Paragraph 1: – Astronomy is becoming popular
– children want books about it and telescopes

Paragraph 2: – people are interested because of recent events:
lunar/solar eclipses, and the Hale-Bopp comet

Paragraph 3: – children watch the sky changing every night
– some hope to find a new comet like Hale and Bopp

Paragraph 4: – some children want to be astronauts
– some children want to become space tourists

Now put the information together to make a four-sentence summary.

Astronomy: a summary ....
....
....
....
....
....

13 Verb forms

Write the correct form of the verb in brackets (Present simple or Present continuous) in the spaces.

a I (live) *live*............. in a big flat.
b Paul (live) .... in a nice house with a garden.
c Maria (eat) .... her dinner at the moment.
d Mike and Dave (play) .... football every Saturday.
e Liz and her mother (go) .... shopping now.
f Jake (not work) .... at present.
g Steve and Angi (not come) .... here on Thursdays.
h Peter (have) .... a birthday party this afternoon.
i He always (have) .... a birthday party every year.
j Judy (go) .... skiing every winter.
k Petra (not like) .... skiing.
l They never (go) .... on holiday in August.
m Chris (have) .... his breakfast in the garden every day.
n We (do) .... our homework this evening.
o Alex (want) .... a new job.
p Why .... you (drink) .... my coffee now?

Unit 2

1 Questions and answers
Make questions starting *What time ... ?* about yesterday. Then answer each one.

a go to school *What time did you go to school yesterday?*
   I went to school at half-past seven.

b wake up
   ....
   ....

c have breakfast
   ....
   ....

d eat lunch
   ....
   ....

e leave school
   ....
   ....

f get home
   ....
   ....

g do your homework
   ....
   ....

h watch TV
   ....
   ....

i go to bed
   ....
   ....

2 When did it happen?
Write about the activities below, and when they happened.

a go swimming? *I went swimming three days ago. I went swimming in January. I went*
   swimming on Tuesday afternoon.

b drink some Coca Cola? ....

c visit your grandmother? ....

d eat a hamburger? ....

e travel on a train? ....

f write a letter? ....

g have a shower/bath? ....

h see a film at the cinema? ....

i ride a bicycle? ....

3 The party
Make questions about a party using the words below.
Give a full answer to each question.

a Who/meet/party? Maria *Who did you meet at the party? I met Maria.*

b When/go/party? eight o'clock

c What/eat/party? pizza

d Who/dance with/party? Paul and Dave

e When/leave/party? eleven o'clock

f How/travel/home? bus

g What time/get/home? quarter to midnight

4 Who did it?
Write a subject and an object question for each sentence. Give a short answer.

a Bill rescued Peter. *Who rescued Peter? Bill.*
Who did Bill rescue? Peter.

b Mary helped her mother.

c Mike and Dave carried the box.

d Sarah listened to the CDs.

e Paul drove the car.

f Steve took the dog out.

5 Vocabulary
Write the correct word from the box in each space. They are all new words from Unit 2.

| voyage | invention | unsafe | arrangements | castaway |
| attempt | uninhabited | performance | talented | audience |

a The scientist made something new. It was his new *invention* .
b They got everything ready for their journey. They made their ....
c He was left alone on the island. He was a ....
d There were no people on the island. It was ....
e He can sing, dance and play the guitar well. He is very ....
f Tonight they have a concert in the theatre. It's their first ....
g I hope lots of people go to the concert. They need a big ....
h He's trying to climb Everest again. It's his second ....
i Don't walk across that old wooden bridge. It's ....
j He went round the world in a small boat. It was a very long ....

6 Prepositions
Choose the correct preposition to fit in each space. You can use some of the words more than once.

| on | in | of | near | from | to |

a Paul lives *on* an island .... the Atlantic Ocean.
b He lives .... a small house made .... wood.
c The house is .... a river.
d Paul eats fruit which he takes out .... the forest.
e In summer he swims .... the river.
f He sometimes climbs .... the top .... the big hill .... the middle of the island.
g .... the hilltop he can see all .... the island.

7a Robinson Crusoe
Read this passage from the story of Robinson Crusoe.

I kept the skins of the animals that I killed for food. The first thing I made out of these was a big cap for my head. The fur was outside so that the rain ran off it. It was very good. I then made myself some other clothes – a jacket with no sleeves and some knee-length short trousers. I made them bigger than I needed. I didn't want to be hot when I wore them, because the weather was very hot on my island. These clothes were not very beautiful, but when it rained they kept me dry.

I also tried to make an umbrella. I needed one to keep both the rain and the sun off me as I had to spend a lot of time outside. I made two or three before I finally made one which was good. I used animal skins to cover it. The most difficult thing was to make it go up and down, so that I could carry it with me. I did it in the end. Then I took my umbrella with me everywhere, and it was useful in both the hottest and the wettest weather.

7b Correct the following statements.

a Robinson Crusoe made clothes from the skins of birds.
No, he made clothes from the skins of animals.

b He killed the animals just for their skins.
....

c The first thing that Crusoe made was an umbrella.
....

d He made his clothes with the hair inside to keep him warm.
....

e The clothes he made looked very good.
....

f The first umbrella Crusoe made was good.
....

g It was easy to make the umbrella go up and down.
....

h Crusoe wanted to use the umbrella only when it rained.
....

8 Labelling a picture
Look at the picture and label the things that Robinson Crusoe made for himself.

cap

9 Telling a story
Put the words in the box into the correct spaces in the story below.
Some of the words can go in more than one space.

| then | next | finally | first of all | after that |

Robinson Crusoe finds fruit on the island

I decided to go and look at the country in the middle of the island. (1) *First of all* I got my boat from the place where I kept it and put it into the river. (2) .... I went up the river for about two kilometres. I left the boat at the side of the river, and (3) .... I walked into the forest. I found lots of different sorts of fruit, which I put into my baskets. (4) .... I walked back to where my boat was.
(5) .... I put the baskets into the boat and went back down the river to where I lived.

10 Guided writing

Now write a short story of your own. Write 100–120 words.
It can be something that really happened to you, or a story that you invent yourself.
Think of what happened first, what happened next, and so on.
Use the words in the box in Exercise 9 to tell your story.

....
....
....
....
....
....
....
....

11 Past simple spelling

Write the Past simple forms of these regular verbs.

- **a** start   *started*
- **b** stop
- **c** work
- **d** study
- **e** stay
- **f** wash
- **g** carry
- **h** ski
- **i** happen
- **j** rescue
- **k** shout
- **l** like
- **m** decide
- **n** practise
- **o** live
- **p** remain

Now group all the words according to how they form the Past simple.

Add 'd'.	Add 'ed'.	Double the consonant, add 'ed'.	Change the 'y' to 'i', add 'ed'.
	start		

Unit 2

Unit 3

1 Questions and answers
Make questions and answers using the Past continuous.

a When I telephoned, what/you/do? play/piano
When I telephoned, what were you doing? I was playing the piano.

b When he arrived, what/she/do? wash/hair
When he arrived, ...

c When the taxi got there, what/they/do? get/dressed
When the taxi got there, ...

d When the match started, what/fans/do? sing/football songs
When the match started, ...

e When you got home, what/your parents/do? go/bed
When you got home, ...

f When it started raining, what/you two/do? walk/park
When it started raining, ...

g When the train came, what/he/do? read/newspaper
When the train came, ...

2 Past continuous 1
Make sentences using the Past continuous and the words below. Start each sentence with *While*.

a Paul/read/Mike/watch TV
While Paul was reading, Mike was watching TV.

b Sue/brush/hair/Jane/have/shower
....

c Mum/clean/car/Dad/cut/grass
....

d the boys/play/basketball/the girls/swim
....

e Steve/do/homework/brother/use/computer
....

f Class 4A/study/Maths/Class 5A/have/Art lesson
....

g my mother/make/cake/my grandmother/cook/lunch
....

16 sixteen

3 Past continuous 2
Make sentences using the Past continuous and the words below.

a I/watch/TV/telephone/ring
   While I was watching TV, the telephone rang.
   or *I was watching TV when the telephone rang.*

b I/eat/dinner/my brother/come/home
   ....
   or ....

c my parents/visit/friends/someone/steal/car
   ....
   or ....

d we/play/football/start/rain
   ....
   or ....

e Robert/ride/bicycle/fall/off
   ....
   or ....

f I/walk/school/meet/friend
   ....
   or ....

g Peter and I/do/homework/lights/go out
   ....
   or ....

4 Vocabulary
Write the correct word from the box in each space. They are all new words from Unit 3.

queue	starve	raid	surrender	view
drought	approach	crashed	~~donate~~	sweep

a I decided to *donate* some of my pocket money to the Red Cross.
b When you are on the top of the hill, the .... is beautiful.
c It hasn't rained for weeks and we are worried that there will be a ....
d Thousands of children in Africa .... to death each year.
e I asked the cleaner to .... the floors again because they were very dirty.
f You must .... the birds very carefully, or they will fly away.
g We had to .... outside the concert hall to see Smart Moves.
h There was an accident and the car .... into the wall.
i The police made a .... on the criminal's house last night.
j The government hopes that the armed men will soon .... to the police.

5 Putting words together
Draw a line from each word in the left-hand column to the word it goes with in the right-hand column.

1	donate	a	voyage
2	fire	b	ring
3	diamond	c	money
4	armed	d	exhibition
5	swimming	e	money
6	art	f	shake
7	milk	g	engine
8	raise	h	costume
9	sea	i	police

6 Writing sentences
Now write five sentences using the pairs of words. Choose which pairs you want to use.

donate/money: Rich countries often donate money to poorer countries.

....
....
....
....
....

7 Articles
Put an article (*a/an/the*) in the spaces, if necessary; leave a space if no article is necessary.

Henry Ford was born in (1) .... 1863 in America. He made his first car in 1896, and started (2) .... company to make (3) .... cars in 1903: (4) .... Ford Motor Company. In 1908 his company made (5) .... world's first cheap car: (6) .... Model T Ford. Over the next 19 years, until they stopped making it, they sold 5 million of (7) .... cars!

In 1913, Ford had (8) .... new idea which changed (9) .... car-making industry: he made his cars with (10) .... line of people working on them. In this way they were quicker to make. He also paid workers in his factory (11) .... good money.

In (12) .... 1930s, people wanted (13) .... fast cars which looked better than Ford's cars, and other American car-makers like General Motors sold more.

8a Read this passage about Babe Zaharias and answer the questions that follow it.

Babe Zaharias

Babe Zaharias was born in the USA in 1914. As a schoolgirl she soon showed how good she was at many different sports. In 1932, when she was eighteen, she won the team title at the US Women's Athletic Championships on her own! She won five of the eight events.

Later, in 1932, she took part in the Olympic Games in Los Angeles. There she won the gold medal for the hurdles and throwing the javelin, and a silver medal in the long jump.

When she stopped taking part in athletics competitions, she started playing golf. By 1947 she was the best woman golfer in the world. When she won the British Women's Championship that year, it was her seventeenth championship in a row.

She started her sporting activities at a time when most people still thought that sport was only for men. But Babe Zaharias was so good that everyone said she played sport 'like a man'. Not only was she very good, but she was also very popular. Her successes were very important in helping to open the door of the sports world to women.

Babe Zaharias died of cancer in 1956.

8b Complete the table with the events of Babe Zaharias's life.

1914	....
1932	....
1932	....
1947	....
1956	....

8c Answer these questions.

a What was unusual about Babe Zaharias's results at the 1932 US Women's Athletics Championships?
   ....

b How many medals did she win in the 1932 Olympic Games?
   ....

c Apart from athletics, what other sport was she very good at?
   ....

d How many golf championships did she win?
   ....

e When she was young, what did people think about women in sport?
   ....

f Why do you think her success was good for women in sport?
   ....

g Write a definition for these words and phrases.
   title: ....
   gold medal: ....
   in a row: ....
   popular: ....
   open the door: ....
   successes: ....

9 Summary writing
   Now write a five-sentence summary of the article on Babe Zaharias.
   Babe Zaharias: a summary ....
   ....
   ....
   ....
   ....
   ....
   ....
   ....
   ....

10 Guided writing
Use the information below to write about the life of Bill Gates. Look at the passage about Babe Zaharias to see how the paragraphs are made, and write in the same way.
Write 100–120 words.

1955	born in USA
1968	writes first computer program
1974	writes the BASIC software program
1975	leaves Harvard University
1977	starts Microsoft Corporation in Seattle
1981	IBM uses Gates' DOS system in personal computers
1990	Microsoft biggest computer software company in the world
1995	makes the Windows system
1996	becomes youngest billionaire in history

Bill Gates

....
....
....
....
....
....
....
....

11 Writing
Now find out about a famous person from your country and write about his/her life. Write 100–120 words.

....
....
....
....
....
....
....
....

Unit 4

1 Adjectives 1: Word associations
Look at the list of adjectives and nouns below. Match the adjectives with the nouns in any pairs that make sense. Write a sentence using each pair.

Adjectives	Nouns
a skilful	1 animal
b creative	2 actress
c dangerous	3 businessman
d beautiful	4 food
e healthy	5 footballer
f rich	6 film
g entertaining	7 artist

a *skilful   footballer   He is the most skilful footballer in the team.*
b ....
c ....
d ....
e ....
f ....
g ....

2 Adjectives 2: Opposites
Look at the adjectives in the left-hand list and draw a line to their opposite in the right-hand list.

1 heavy	a difficult
2 easy	b bad
3 cold	c short
4 good	d light
5 cheap	e slow
6 tall	f little
7 fast	g sad
8 old	h hot
9 happy	i young
10 big	j expensive

3 Comparatives of adjectives 1: Simple comparisons
Make sentences comparing the two people/things.

a nice/Sarah/Maria   *Sarah is nice, but Maria is nicer.*

b old/Granny Woods/Granny Jones
   ....

c comfortable/this chair/that chair
   ....

d unhealthy/Coke/coffee
   ....

e fast/Mercedes/Ferrari
   ....

f high/Mont Blanc/Mount Everest
   ....

g dangerous/skiing/climbing
   ....

h hot/Greece/Egypt
   ....

i skilful/David Beckham/Luis Figo
   ....

4 Comparatives of adjectives 2: Questions and answers
Ask questions and give short answers about the things below.

a Mont Blanc/Mount Everest/high   *Is Mont Blanc higher than Mount Everest?*
   No, it isn't.

b the USA/the UK/big
   ....
   ....

c the Arctic/Poland/cold
   ....
   ....

d elephant/giraffe/tall
   ....
   ....

e dog/cat/strong
   ....
   ....

f Africa/Europe/hot
   ....
   ....

5a Comparatives of adjectives 3
Complete these sentences with the correct comparative.

a Susan's *happy*, but Mary's *happier* .
b This book's *good*, but that one's ....
c Budapest's a *big* city, but London's ....
d Paul is a *bad* boy, but his brother's ....
e She's a *lucky* girl, but I'm ....
f My dad's *fat*, but your dad's ....
g The book I bought is *large*, but there are many that are ....
h The last James Bond film was *interesting*, but the new one is ....
i He runs *fast*, but she runs ....

5b Write a sentence to describe the changes you made.

a fast: *You add -er to the adjective.*
b happy/lucky: ....
c good/bad: ....
d big/fat: ....
e large: ....
f interesting: ....

6 Superlatives of adjectives
Make sentences using the words below and the superlative.

a this/tall/tree/forest   *This is the tallest tree in the forest.*
b that/comfortable/chair/room   ....
c he/nice/person/know   ....
d that/old/house/town   ....
e she/beautiful/girl/school   ....
f he/short/boy/class   ....
g this/expensive/book/shop   ....
h they/good/band/world   ....
i it/lovely/song/know   ....
j it/useful/thing/have   ....
k he/exciting/player/team   ....

Unit 4

7 Comparing three things
Look at the information and compare the three people/things.

a Dave: 1.35 m/Mike: 1.31 m/me: 1.28 m
I'm tall, Mike is taller, but Dave is the tallest.

b Jill: 65 kg/Angi: 68 kg/me: 72 kg

c Mercedes: $30,000/Porsche: $32,000/Ferrari: $38,000

d Dick: 18 yrs/Jack: 19 yrs/me: 20 yrs

e Edinburgh: 2 °C/Oslo: 0 °C/Rekjavik: −3 °C

f Lada: 95 kph/Wartburg: 88 kph/Trabant: 77 kph

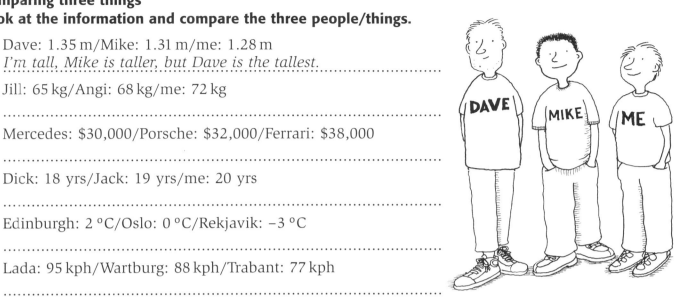

8 Vocabulary
Write the correct word from the box in each space.
They are all new words from Unit 4.

| size | brightened up | waterfall | ancestors | brains |
| hunted | climate | creatures | axe | previous |

a The *climate* here is beautiful: it's not too hot in summer, and not too cold in winter.
b One of my .... was a very famous scientist.
c What .... shirt do you usually wear? This one looks too big.
d We walked along the river, and came to a .... where the water came down about 20 metres.
e We use our .... to think about things.
f John went to get his .... to cut up the wood for the fire.
g We watched as the lion .... the other animals.
h It was raining all morning, but it .... in the afternoon.
i I didn't think that goal was as good as the .... one.
j The .... that live in the forest are different from those that live in the mountains.

twenty five 25

9 Reading
Read this passage about early people in Hungary.

One of the most important prehistoric places in Europe is near Tata, about 70 kilometres west of Budapest in Hungary. Here, in 1965, archaeologists found the bones of a *homo erectus* ('standing man'), and called him 'Samuel'!

This was a very exciting place for the archaeologists because, as well as the human bones, they also found the place he camped in, with the tools he made from stones, a camp fire, and the bones of the animals he killed for food.

From the things that they found, the archaeologists say that this man was first there between 350 and 400 thousand years ago. They know this because of the size of his brain and the tools they found.

He lived in a very good place – there were warm rivers, and the climate was very nice. His children and their children lived here for hundreds of years, and it is possible to see how his tools changed and became better over a long period of time.

Decide if these sentences are true (T) or false (F).

- a ..F.. : 'Samuel' was the prehistoric man's name.
- b ...... : Samuel was found in Budapest.
- c ...... : Samuel is an example of 'homo erectus'.
- d ...... : 'Homo erectus' means 'a man who can stand up'.
- e ...... : The archaeologists only found the bones of the prehistoric man near Tata.
- f ...... : Samuel knew how to make fire.
- g ...... : The archaeologists know in exactly which years Samuel was alive.
- h ...... : The area near Tata where Samuel lived was difficult to live in.
- i ...... : Prehistoric people lived in that area for a long time.

10 Summary writing

Now write a summary of the article about Samuel on p. 26. There are four short paragraphs. Write just one sentence to summarise each paragraph.

Samuel: a summary ....
....
....
....
....
....

11 Writing

Think about what life was like for the first humans. Reread the passages on 'Early Humans' in the *Student's Book* and on 'Samuel' above. Try to think how they lived. What did they do every day? What problems did they have? What were the good things about their life? What made them happy and sad? Then write about 100 words on what you think their daily life was like.

Life for Early Humans ....
....
....
....
....
....
....

Unit 5

1 Future predictions 1
Make predictions about what will happen, using sentences with *will*.

- a bus/late — *I think the bus will be late.*
- b bus/not/late — *I don't think the bus will be late.*
- c Susan/win/match ....
- d they/not/come ....
- e Dad/be home/soon ....
- f the teacher/give us/homework ....
- g he/not/finish/the work ....
- h it/rain/tomorrow ....
- i she/ride/her bike/to school ....
- j they/not/build/the wall/today ....

2 Future predictions 2
There are different ways to say how sure we are about future events. Look at this:

not very sure			very sure
Perhaps it will …	It will probably …	I expect it will …	It will definitely …
Perhaps it won't …	It probably won't …	I expect it won't …	It definitely won't …
	rain all day tomorrow.		

Think about the future in your life and make some predictions. Write an affirmative sentence when you see (+) and a negative sentence when you see (–). Use the words in brackets.

- a (+ : probably)   *Tomorrow I will probably visit my grandmother.*
- b (– : definitely) *Tomorrow I definitely won't visit my grandmother.*
- c (+ : perhaps)   Tomorrow ....
- d (+ : probably)   Next Saturday ....
- e (+ : expect)   On Monday ....
- f (+ : definitely) Next holidays ....
- g (– : perhaps)   When I'm 18 ....
- h (– : probably)   On Sunday afternoon ....
- i (– : expect)   This evening ....
- j (– : definitely) Tomorrow morning ....

3 Questions and answers
Make questions using the words below. Give a short answer to each question.

a you/at school/tomorrow?   *Will you be at school tomorrow? Yes, I will.*
b friend/meet you/tomorrow?   ....
c you/black shoes/tomorrow?   ....
d mother/dinner/tonight?   ....
e you/sport/next Saturday?   ....
f best friend/your house/weekend?   ....
g you/disco/Friday night?   ....
h English teacher/test/tomorrow?   ....
i you/bed/early/tonight?   ....

4 Making promises
Use the cues to make the requests and promises.

a Teacher: homework/tonight   *Do your homework tonight.*
   Student: do it   *I'll do it.*
b Mother: not home/late   ....
   Daughter: home/early   ....
c Girlfriend: meet/8 p.m.   ....
   Boyfriend: be/on time   ....
d Teacher: walk/corridor   ....
   Pupil: not run/corridor   ....
e Father: play/music/quietly   ....
   Son: not/play/music/loud   ....
f Girl: bring/my CD/back   ....
   Friend: not forget/tomorrow   ....
g Mother: find/football shirt   ....
   Son: find it/tonight   ....
h Friend 1: not miss/bus/tomorrow   ....
   Friend 2: catch it   ....

5 Saying the right thing
What would you say in these situations?

You can use the verbs in the box.

buy   show   give   get

a Your friend hasn't got a pencil in class.
   ....

b You're playing football and someone kicks the ball into the next garden.
   ....

c Your mother has forgotten to buy some eggs. She's very tired.
   ....

d Your friend doesn't know how to get to the party. She has a map.
   ....

6 Vocabulary
Write the correct word from the box in each space. They are all new words from Unit 5.

crowded	recognise	factory	polluted	~~appearance~~
replace	tidy	resolution	borrow	lawn

a I saw from his ...*appearance*........ that he had no money or home.
b What do they make in that .... ? Car engines?
c Can I .... your Britney Spears CD for the evening, please?
d I didn't .... my brother when he came to the party in a suit!
e After I saw that TV programme, I made a .... to stop smoking.
f My mother doesn't like my bedroom! She always tells me to .... it!
g I went to the disco on Friday, but I soon left because it was very ....
h There are traffic jams so often in this town that the air is very ....
i I'm sorry, John. I broke your new CD, but I'll .... it for you tomorrow.
j Dad's out in the back garden cutting the ....

7a Read the following passage.

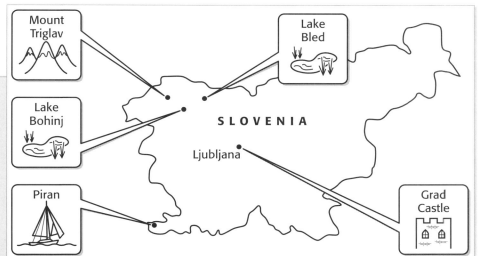

Holidays in Slovenia

I already know where I'll go for my next holidays. Not Barbados, not Egypt, nor the Seychelles. I'm not even going to visit the more usual holiday destinations like a Greek island, Tuscany in Italy or the Spanish coast. No, I'll go to Slovenia. Many people in Europe don't really know where Slovenia is … which is very good for me, because it means that there aren't so many tourists!

I will fly to Brnik, just outside the capital, Ljubljana, and collect my car. After that I'll do what I feel like, because nothing else is planned. I expect I'll stay in Ljubljana for two or three days because it's a very pretty city. It has a river running through the middle of it and lots of nice pavement cafés. It's full of interesting old buildings, and from the Grad Castle on the hill you get a beautiful view across the city.

After that, if the weather is good, I'll probably drive up to the mountains. I'll spend some time near Lake Bled or Lake Bohinj. They're right under Mount Triglav which, at 2,864 metres, is Slovenia's highest mountain. Perhaps I'll walk in the mountains on some days, and drive around and look at the pretty fields and farms on others.

Then I'll definitely go down to the Adriatic coast and stay in Piran. The coast is lovely – pretty villages, blue water and lots of good fish to eat and white wine to drink with it. I'll spend a week relaxing, and enjoying the sea air.

Then it will be time to drive slowly back to Ljubljana for a last night or two before flying back home. You see, for such a small country, Slovenia has everything for a good holiday – mountains, seaside, interesting towns and fewer tourists than other nice places!

7b Now answer these questions.

a Why does the writer say that Slovenia is a better place to go for a holiday than Tuscany or the Greek islands?

....

b Describe two things which the writer feels make Ljubljana a pretty city.

....

c What will help the writer decide whether to go to stay near Triglav?

....

d Describe two things which the writer will enjoy at Piran.

....

e What does the writer feel is surprising about the size of Slovenia?

....

8 Summary writing

Write a summary of the passage about Slovenia. There are five paragraphs. Write one sentence to summarise each paragraph. Write in the third person singular (*he knows* … *he'll go* …).

Holidays in Slovenia: a summary

9 Guided writing

Write about a good place for a holiday that you know.
Imagine that you'll go there for your next holiday. Say what you'll probably and definitely do. Give information about the place, and say what is attractive there. Use the passage about Slovenia as a model.
Write about 100 words.

A good place for a holiday

10 Prepositions
Put one preposition into each space in the text below.

When I visited the planet of Trigon-X5 for the first time, they immediately took me to a strange building.

When I walked (1) .... the room I was very surprised. There were no people (2) .... it, just a lot (3) .... robots. Some robots were sitting (4) .... desks, working (5) .... computers, while others were talking (6) .... some strange animals (7) .... the large videophones. It was just like a normal office, except (8) .... the robots. I walked (9) .... where one robot was writing (10) .... a computer screen.

'What are you doing?' I asked.

The robot didn't answer me. I looked (11) .... my host.

'The robots (12) .... this department aren't programmed to speak to humans,' he said. 'Come (13) .... me and I'll show you some others.'

We walked (14) .... (15) .... the room and visited another office.

11 Articles
Read more about life on Trigon-X5. Put an article in the spaces, if necessary.

(1) .... next office was very different. On (2) .... door was (3) .... sign saying 'Programming Office'. Inside there was (4) .... large green robot sitting at (5) .... big orange desk. In front of (6) .... green robot were many rows of (7) .... desks and chairs. It looked like (8) .... very big Earth classroom.

'What's (9) .... green robot doing?' I asked.

'It's waiting for (10) .... student robots to come in,' he answered. 'It's (11) .... first programming class of (12) .... school year.'

Just then, there was (13) .... noise at (14) .... back of (15) .... room, and about (16) .... hundred small green robots came in. Each one stood behind (17) .... small red chair and waited until (18) .... electronic bell rang. Then all (19) .... robots sat down on (20) .... red chairs.

Stopover One

1 Past simple or Past continuous? Choose the correct alternatives.

Last Saturday, while I (1) *was walking/walked* down the road, I (2) *was seeing/saw* someone I (3) *thought/was thinking* was at the same school as me: Robert Smith. We were quite good friends at school, but when we (4) *studied/were studying* at different universities we (5) *were stopping/stopped* meeting. Robert (6) *walked/was walking* quickly along the street, so I (7) *was deciding/decided* to follow him, which was difficult because a lot of people (8) *did/were doing* their shopping. After a minute or two I (9) *was seeing/saw* him go into a big shop selling electrical equipment – TVs, computers, mobile phones, and so on. I (10) *was entering/entered* the shop and soon (11) *noticed/was noticing* Robert over near the computer area of the shop, so I (12) *was going/went* towards him. When I (13) *was getting/got* near him, I (14) *saw/was seeing* him look carefully around the shop, and when there were no assistants near, he (15) *was putting/put* a small hand-held computer into his pocket. Then he (16) *looked/was looking* at me, and (17) *was putting/put* his finger to his mouth to say 'Sshh! Be quiet!' I (18) *wasn't knowing/didn't know* what to do. Robert (19) *went/was going* out of the shop very quickly. When I (20) *got/was getting* out into the street, Robert wasn't there.

2 Time words
Complete each sentence with a word from the box.

| ago | in | on | last | at | next |

a What were you doing .... ten o'clock .... night?
b I first went to London five years ....
c Lessons start .... 9 o'clock .... the morning.
d Where will Paul be .... week?
e John had his 10th birthday .... 2000.
f His birthday is .... 1st January.
g He will be in France .... the evening.
h What do you want to do .... week?

Stopover One

3 Making comparisons
Make comparisons using the adjectives given.

a comfortable
Shorts are more comfortable than trousers.

b cheap
....

c slow
....

d loud
....

4 Making sentences with superlatives
Use the words below to write sentences with superlatives about the people in your class.

a tall/boy *Peter is the tallest boy in my class.*
b clever/girl ....
c interesting/person ....
d short/girl ....
e heavy/boy ....
f good/student of English ....
g good/friend ....

Unit 6

1 **Present perfect simple: Affirmative and negative**
Make affirmative (+) or negative (−) Present perfect sentences using the words below.

a he/take/another chocolate (+)   *He's taken another chocolate.*
b he/take/another chocolate (−)   *He hasn't taken another chocolate.*
c she/visit/London (+) ....
d they/buy/a new house (−) ....
e he/see/the latest film (−) ....
f she/play/computer chess (+) ....
g they/lose/all their matches (+) ....
h Mary/go/to India (+) ....
i the boys/eat/pizza (−) ....
j John/put/his rollerblades away (−) ....
k the girls/make/their beds (+) ....
l the dog/have/its food (−) ....
m he/watch/new DVD (−) ....
n she/buy/some Levi jeans (+) ....

2 **The last two hours**

Draw the time now: **Draw the time two hours ago:**

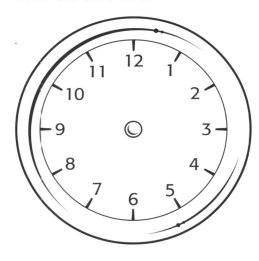 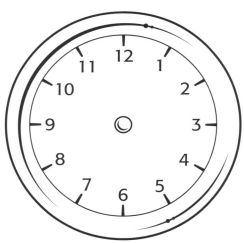

Now think: What have you/haven't you done in the last two hours? Make a list of six things.

a *I've* ....
b ....
c ....
d ....
e ....
f ....

3 Present perfect simple: Making questions (regular verbs)
Make *Have you/they ever ...?* or *Has he/she ever ...?* questions using the words below.

a you/work/farm? *Have you ever worked on a farm?*
b he/clean/his car?
c she/talk/an Englishman?
d they/wash/the dog?
e you/collect/stamps?
f she/paint/a picture?
g they/want/a cat?
h she/watch/*Titanic*?
i you/cook/pizza?
j he/listen/Beethoven's Fifth Symphony?
k you/visit/London?
l they/live/abroad?

4 Present perfect simple: Making questions (irregular verbs)
Make *Have you ever ...?* questions using the words below.
Give a short answer to each question.

a eat/spaghetti? *Have you ever eaten spaghetti? Yes, I have.*
b go/England?
c see/*Gladiator*?
d ride/horse?
e make/cake?
f lose/keys?
g sleep/all day?
h drink/whisky?
i speak/Italian?
j fall/bike?
k run/1 km?
l write/a poem?
m read/*Financial Times*?
n send/e-mail?
o forget/to do homework?

5 Never
Write five things that you have never done.

a *I've never visited New York.*
b ....
c ....
d ....
e ....
f ....

6 Just and yet
Make sentences using *just* and *yet*.

a It's 5 o'clock. He's not home. *He hasn't come home yet.*
b It's 5 o'clock. He arrived home two minutes ago. *He's just come home.*
c The lesson started five minutes ago. Paul is not in class.
   ....
d It's midnight at Peter's New Year's Eve party. The champagne bottle is open.
   ....
e The football match finished five minutes ago. It was Liverpool 2–Leeds 1.
   ....
f It's bedtime, but my English homework is unfinished.
   ....
g It's time to go to school, but John is in bed.
   ....
h The film starts in five minutes. Sue is not in the cinema.
   ....
i The exam finishes in one minute. Dave is writing answers.
   ....
j It's 12 o'clock. The teacher is collecting the exam papers.
   ....

Unit 6

7 Been and gone
Look at these two sentences:

Mike has just left the house with two empty shopping bags.   He's gone to the shops.
Mike has just come home with two bags full of shopping.   He's been to the shops.

Now write similar sentences with been or gone.

a It's four o'clock. Susan's just come home with her schoolbag.
   ....

b It's 9 o'clock in the morning. Mr Brown has just left the house with his briefcase.
   ....

c The boys are in a café talking about the film they've just seen.
   ....

d The girls have just left the house with their swimming costumes.
   ....

e Peter's coming home from the café, and he's feeling full.
   ....

8 Vocabulary
Write the correct word from the box in each space.
They are all new words from Unit 6.

sauce	tractor	cause	petrol	melted
level	disappear	waste	wallet	plant

a The magician was very good. He took a rabbit from his hat, then made it *disappear* .
b The farmer bought a new .... for his farm.
c I went to the Police Station because I lost my .... with all my money in it.
d I left my chocolate in the sun and it ....
e I love to eat tomato .... with my fish and chips.
f Write on both sides or you will .... the paper.
g If we use cars too much, we will .... the city to get polluted.
h It hasn't rained for a long time. The .... of water in the lake has gone down.
i I hope your new car uses green ....
j I've bought some beautiful roses to .... in the back garden.

thirty nine 39

9a Read the passage.

Drinking and Health

Scientists have found out that most people do not drink enough water. It is very important to drink between eight and ten glasses every day. Not drinking enough water is the Number One cause of people being tired at work or at school.

If you cannot understand how to do a Maths problem, or you cannot see your computer screen or the page of a book very well, drink a glass of water. Some scientists also think that if you drink five glasses of water every day, you will have fewer health problems (including cancer) when you are older.

It is well known that popular fizzy drinks are bad for your teeth. Recently, scientists have also said that some types of fizzy drinks are bad for other parts of the body. Try this: put a small piece of metal into a glass of your favourite drink and leave it for about five days. It will start to disappear. If it can do that to metal, think what it can do to your body!

Another drink that scientists have written about is coffee. It smells wonderful, it tastes wonderful, but it is very bad for you. It has 17 different 'toxins' in it which can cause lots of problems for your body.

So start drinking lots of water and cut down on (or better cut out!) fizzy drinks and coffee. Always read what it says on the side of the bottle before drinking anything – if it has sugar in it, you don't need it. Drink green tea if you want a hot drink – it protects the body from serious illnesses. If you want something fruity, drink small amounts of 100% juice mixed with water.

9b Write a short answer to each sentence, agreeing or disagreeing with what it says.

a It is very important to be careful what we drink. _Yes, it is._
b Most people drink less water than they need. ....
c Everybody needs to drink five glasses every day. ....
d Not drinking enough water is one of the causes of people feeling tired. ....
e Drinking a lot of water can help people not to get ill when they are older. ....
f Scientists say fizzy drinks and coffee are dangerous for the human body. ....
g You must always drink drinks with sugar in them. ....
h You should put water into 100% fruit juice before you drink it. ....
i Green tea is also good for us. ....
j Toxins are good for your body. ....
k What tastes good is always good for you. ....
l I will try to drink enough water each day from now on. ....

Unit 6

9c Look at these words and phrases from the article 'Drinking and Health'. Write a short definition for each one.

a scientist: *A scientist is a person who studies science.*
b computer screen: ....
c cancer: ....
d fizzy drink: ....
e wonderful: ....
f cut down on: ....

10 Summary writing
Write a summary of the 'Drinking and Health' passage.
There are five paragraphs. Write a sentence summarising each paragraph.

Drinking and Health: a summary

....
....
....
....
....
....

11 Guided writing
Now write about 'Food and Health'. Think about the things we eat that are bad for us: sweet things, things with too much fat in them, and so on. Decide what problems they cause for the human body. Also think about what food is good for us and why. Organise your paragraphs like the 'Drinking and Health' passage.
Write 100–120 words.

Food and Health

....
....
....
....
....
....

Unit 7

1. **Can and may**
   We use *can* and *may* to ask permission to do things. *May* is more formal than *can*.
   Make the following requests, and answer them with a positive (+) or negative (−) answer.
   Remember to use *please* in both types of request.

   a informal: go/cinema/tomorrow   *Can I go to the cinema tomorrow, please?*
      (−)   *No, you can't.*

   b informal: visit/grandmother/tomorrow ....
      (+)   ....

   c formal: help/school party   ....
      (+)   ....

   d informal: go/Paul's party/tonight ....
      (−)   ....

   e formal: work/outside/this afternoon ....
      (−)   ....

   f formal: get/my ball/your garden ....
      (+)   ....

   g informal: have/fish/dinner   ....
      (+)   ....

   h formal: borrow/your book/this evening ....
      (+)   ....

2. **One/ones**
   Write answers to the questions using *like(d)* and *one/ones*.

   a Do you like the **red** pullover? (**blue**)
      No, I like the blue one.

   b Shall I buy you the **grey** trousers? (**black**)
      No, ...

   c And what about those **black** shoes? (**brown**)
      ....

   d I like that **blue** jacket. Let's buy that. (**green**)
      ....

   e Do you like **this** story by Roald Dahl? (**that**)
      ....

   f Did you enjoy the **new** Di Caprio film? (**previous**)
      ....

   g Do you want the **Swiss** cheese for dinner? (**French**)
      ....

3 Shopping
Use the words in the box to complete the dialogue below.

| cost | 34 | big | May | take | light | How much |
| nice | expensive | size | medium | £8.99 | one | cheaper |

Janet: (1) *May* I see that jacket in the window, please?
Assistant: What (2) .... do you take?
Janet: I usually take a (3) .... What size is that one?
Assistant: It's a 38, I'm afraid, so it's too (4) .... for you.
Janet: Oh, OK. Have you got any (5) .... -size pullovers?
Assistant: Yes, we've got these new ones over here.
Janet: I like them. They're very (6) .... May I try the red (7) .... on, please?
Assistant: Yes, certainly. The fitting room is there.
(*Later*) How is it?
Janet: It's just right. (8) .... is it?
Assistant: It's £18.50.
Janet: Oh dear, that's very (9) ....
Assistant: Well, these ones are (10) ....
Janet: Oh, I like this (11) .... green one. How much does it (12) .... ?
Assistant: It's only (13) ....
Janet: Right. I'll (14) .... that one, please.

4 Prepositions
Put one preposition into each of the spaces.

Last year I stayed (1) ..*at*.. a lovely hotel (2) .... Scotland. I heard about it (3) .... a friend who stayed there the year before.

I went there (4) .... my friend Paul. We drove (5) .... Scotland and then didn't use the car much (6) .... that. The people who worked (7) .... the hotel were very friendly, and the room I slept (8) .... was very nice: it had a lovely view (9) .... the hills. Paul could see the sea (10) .... his room. Each morning and evening we went (11) .... the hotel restaurant to eat, and all the food (12) .... the menu was very good.

5 Possession
Look at the pictures and write the questions and answers correctly.

a *Whose bag is this?*
   Is it Paul's?
   No, it's his.

b ....
   ....
   ....

c ....
   ....
   ....

d ....
   ....
   ....

e ....
   ....
   ....

f ....
   ....
   ....

g ....
   ....
   ....

6 You're allowed/not allowed to
Look at the signs below and write a *You're allowed/not allowed to* sentence next to them.

a NO RUNNING NEAR POOL — *You're not allowed to run near the pool.*
b NO PARKING IN FRONT OF GATES — ....
c NO SMOKING ON PLANE — ....
d PICNIC AREA — ....
e NO DOGS IN RESTAURANT — ....
f NO NOISE AFTER 11 p.m. — ....
g PETS WELCOME IN HOTEL — ....
h NO SKATEBOARDING IN PLAYGROUND — ....

7a Sports rules
Match the sports on the left and the list of things you're not allowed to do on the right.

Sport		Not allowed to …	
1	basketball	a	pass the ball forward
2	tennis	b	walk without bouncing the ball
3	volleyball	c	hit the ball behind you
4	baseball	d	catch the ball in your hands
5	rugby	e	hit the net with your racket

7b Write some sentences like this.

1/b: *In basketball you're not allowed to walk without bouncing the ball.*
2/__: ....
3/__: ....
4/__: ....
5/__: ....

7c What other sports rules do you know? Write some more below.

a ....
b ....
c ....

8a Look at the rules for these two hotels.

RULES

Breakfast 08.00 to 09.00 only

Hot showers on Tuesdays and Saturdays only

No noise after 11 p.m.

No pets of any kind in rooms

Guests must leave by 09.30

Payment in cash only

No children under 12

No parking in front of hotel

RULES

Breakfast from 07.00 to 10.00

Dinner from 19.00 to 22.30

Hot running water in all rooms

No noise after 11 p.m.

No dogs in rooms

Guests must leave by 12.00

Payment by credit card, cheque or in cash

Families welcome

Car park at rear of hotel

Enjoy your stay with us!

8b Now answer these questions.

a Which hotel has the longest breakfast time? How long is it?

....

b Can you have dinner at the Gridlock Hotel?

....

c Do they like children at the Happystay Hotel?

....

d Which hotel has more ways of paying? How many ways does it have?

....

e Which hotel do you think sounds best? Why?

....

9 Summary writing

Write a paragraph (about 100 words) in which you summarise the rules of ONE of the two hotels on p. 46. Use phrases like these: *You can/can't, You must/mustn't, You're allowed to/not allowed to.*

Hotel rules: a summary ....
....
....
....
....
....

10 Guided writing

Write about a sport or game that you like playing or watching. Include: how many people play on each side; what clothes and equipment they need; the object of the game; the most important rules; how long the game takes; where you play it. Write about 100 words.

How to play ....
....
....
....
....
....
....
....

11 Vocabulary

Write the correct word from the box in each space. They are all new words from Unit 7.

receipt	luggage	plenty	include	aware
~~entry~~	towels	Hang	label	huge

a You have to pay a £10 *entry*........... fee to get into the new Sports Centre.
b What do you get when you pay £10? What does that payment .... ?
c 'Are you .... that you are not allowed to park here, sir?' asked the policeman.
d There are .... of other shops we can go to if you don't like the shirts here.
e In a shop they give you a .... for things you have bought.
f The .... in this hotel are so small that I can't dry myself with them!
g Oh, I'm fine! I brought a .... towel with me – I know what hotels are like!
h .... your coat up behind the door, and come into the sitting room.
i 'What size is this pullover?' 'I don't know – read what it says on the ....'
j I'm sorry, but you can only take one piece of hand .... onto the plane.

Unit 8

1 Past simple or Present perfect? 1
In English, conversations usually move from a question in the
Present perfect to a question in the Past simple, like this:

Have you ever seen a Smart Moves concert?

When did you see it?

Yes, I have.

I saw it last year.

Now complete these conversations in the same way.

a go/London   John: ....
                          Paul: Yes, I have.
    when/go   John: ....
    go/last summer   Paul: ....

b eat/kangaroo   Liz: ....
                          Jane: Yes, I have.
    where/eat   Liz: ....
    visit/Australia   Jane: ....

c drink/champagne   Steve: ....
                          Mike: Yes, I have.
    when/drink   Steve: ....
    go/brother's wedding Mike: ....

d sleep/tent   Sally: ....
                          Angi: Yes, I have.
    where/sleep/tent   Sally: ....
    be/holiday/Italy   Angi: ....

e meet/famous person Bill: ....
                          Maria: Yes, I have.
    who/meet   Bill: ....
    meet/Robbie Williams Maria: ....

f swim/sea   Linda: ....
                          Dick: Yes, I have.
    where/swim/sea   Linda: ....
    swim/sea/Spain   Dick: ....

2 Past simple or Present perfect? 2
Write questions using either the Present perfect (no specific time) or the Past simple (specific time or place) and the words below. Then give a short answer to each one.

a you/eat/kangaroo? *Have you ever eaten kangaroo? Yes, I have.*
b you/eat/kangaroo/Australia? *Did you eat kangaroo when you were in Australia? Yes I did.*
c you/visit/Venice? ....
d your mother/watch/TV/yesterday? ....
e you/do/homework/at lunchtime? ....
f you get/home/late last night? ....
g your best friend/go/school/last week? ....
h your parents/swim/sea? ....
i you/see/an international match live? ....
j you/read/*Harry Potter* book? ....
k you/get up/7 o'clock/this morning? ....
l your parents/play/computer games? ....

3a The passage below has been written in separate sentences. Read it through.

A Doctor's Life

a John Williams has been a children's doctor for 20 years.
b For the last ten years he has worked for the International Red Cross.
c In that time John has travelled round the world helping young people.
d He has visited Africa, India, South America and South-East Asia.
e He has made over 250 aeroplane journeys for his work.
f Last year John went to five different countries in Africa.
g Children there had many serious health problems.
h There wasn't enough water or food in Somalia.
i There were floods in Mozambique.
j John helped the children in Sudan for six months.

3b Write a question about the information in each sentence in the passage. Start with the question words given.

a How long *has John Williams been a children's doctor?* ....
b Who ....
c Where ....
d Which ....
e How many ....
f Where ....
g What ....
h Where ....
i What ....
j Who ....

4 Answering questions
Think about the last time you went on holiday or away from home.
Answer these questions about what you did there.

Example: Where did you go?   *I went to Prague.* ....

a Where did you go?   ....
b Have you been there before?   ....
c Who did you go with?   ....
d Have you known them for long?   ....
e How did you travel there?   ....
f What did you eat there?   ....
g Have you eaten that before?   ....
h What did you visit there?   ....
i When did you come home?   ....
j What have you done since then?   ....

5 Personal sentences
Look at these two sentences. The first one is a Present perfect sentence about sport, and the second one is a Past simple sentence about places.

Sport (x): I've never played football, but I've played basketball.
Place (y): I went to Prague last year, and I went to Budapest.

Now write type (x) or type (y) sentences of your own about each of these topics.

a Sport (y): ....
b Place (x): ....
c Animal (x): ....
d Transport (y): ....
e School (y): ....
f Music (x): ....
g Holiday (y): ....
h Person (x): ....

6 Infinitive of purpose
Match the two sets of words. Write sentences using the infinitive of purpose and the matched pairs.

a David/go/library   1 watch/match
b Susan/go/shop   2 cook/dinner
c Mike/go/dentist   3 buy/milk
d John/go/stadium   4 catch/train
e Paul/go/kitchen   5 borrow/book
f Jane/go/station   6 play/friends
g Liz/go/park   7 have/check-up
h Angie/go/pool   8 do/shopping
i Sam/go/town   9 practise/swimming

a *David went to the library to borrow a book.*
b ....
c ....
d ....
e ....
f ....
g ....
h ....
i ....

7 Vocabulary
Write the correct word from the box in each space. They are all new words from Unit 8.

| Local | ~~nervous~~ | shy | serious | improve |
| event | industry | damage | mention | freeze |

a I always feel very *nervous* before an exam at school.
b The car .... has caused many of the world's pollution problems.
c It was cold enough last night to .... the river in our town.
d .... people are very angry because the government wants to build a new road here.
e If the government builds the road, it will .... the countryside in this area.
f I find it difficult to make new friends because I'm very ....
g John is a very .... student; he always studies hard before the exams.
h Your homework is not very good, Liz. You must work hard to ....
i Don't .... the story I told you to anyone!
j There are many things happening here this week, but the Smart Moves concert is the most important ....

8a Read this passage.

Making Problems

There are many natural problems which people have to face in the world, including earthquakes, volcanoes and the weather. For example, in early 2001 an earthquake in northern India killed hundreds of people and destroyed the houses of thousands more.

But humans make these problems worse. The floods in Britain and Italy in autumn 2000 and in eastern Hungary and the Ukraine in March 2001 were partly caused by people cutting down trees, changing the direction of rivers and building houses in unsafe places.

Many of our worst weather problems are now caused by global warming – the 'greenhouse effect' – a result of the gases from our industries and cars. The temperature of the Earth is rising, and this changes the weather, causing heavier rain which then causes floods. Also the ice and snow at the North and South Poles are melting, which makes the level of the oceans rise, and this will soon make problems for people who live near the sea.

Governments need to take care of the countries they control and not allow people to do things which change nature. They also need to stop polluting the environment by building more and more factories. If they don't, they will make more problems for our children's children. We can help, too, by using our cars less.

8b Complete these sentences about the passage in your own words.

a There are many natural problems which *people have to face* .
b .... are examples of natural problems which people face.
c There was a terrible .... in India in 2001.
d In Italy, there were bad floods ....
e Many of the .... were caused by cutting down trees and changing the direction of rivers.
f The Earth's temperature is increasing because of ....
g At the Poles the .... and .... are melting.
h When the Poles melt, there is a rise in ....
i Both the governments and the people need to ....

9 Summary writing

Write a summary of the 'Making Problems' passage. Write one sentence to summarise each of the four paragraphs. You do not need to write about the examples of each problem.

Making Problems: a summary

....

....

....

....

....

10 Guided writing

Write about how we can help to make the world less polluted and stop the problems we are making. Start by saying what some of the problems are, then talk about the things we can do. Mention ways in which children like you can help. Write 100 words.

Helping our Earth

....

....

....

....

....

....

....

11 Articles

Put an article (*a/an/the*) in the spaces, if necessary; leave a space if no article is necessary.

When I went to (1) .... England, I visited all (2) .... important places in London. We stayed in (3) .... centre of the city for (4) .... week, and then we went on (5) .... bus tour. At Oxford we saw (6) .... famous old university and at Stratford, (7) .... house where Shakespeare was born. (8) .... weather was very nice. It was (9) .... surprise! Everyone says that (10) .... English weather is always bad. While we were travelling we stayed in (11) .... old hotels in (12) .... small towns. They were very pretty, and made (13) .... change from (14) .... usual international hotels people stay in. We enjoyed (15) .... trip very much indeed.

Unit 9

1. **Questions and answers 1**
   Write some questions and answers about future plans using the words below and the Present continuous.

   a what/do/Saturday/afternoon? — *What are you doing on Saturday afternoon?*
      go/cinema/Peter — *I'm going to the cinema with Peter.*

   b what/do/Friday/night?
      go/disco/friends

   c what/watch/TV/tonight?
      watch/spy film/parents

   d where/go/Sunday morning?
      go/football match/brother

   e where/stay/summer holiday?
      stay/seaside/family

   f what/do/tomorrow evening?
      go/Smart Moves concert/sister

   g how/travel/seaside/tomorrow?
      taking the train/there/Andrew

2. **Questions and answers 2**
   Make questions using Present continuous for the future.
   Give positive (+) or negative (−) short answers.

   a you/go/school/tomorrow? (+) — *Are you going to school tomorrow? Yes, I am.*

   b he/play/football/Saturday? (+)

   c they/come/party/Friday? (−)

   d she/sing/concert/tomorrow? (+)

   e you/go/mountains/weekend? (−)

   f she/visit/grandmother/tonight? (+)

   g they/work/office/weekend? (+)

3 Making suggestions

We can use different structures to make suggestions for future actions.
Use the words given to complete the dialogue below.

Example: Let's/go/theatre   *Let's go to the theatre.*
Why/go/theatre?   *Why don't we go to the theatre?*
What/go/theatre?   *What about going to the theatre?*

Mary: What are you doing on Saturday afternoon?
Sue: Nothing. Why?
Mary: Let's/go/park   ....
Sue: No, the weather's not very nice.
Mary: What/go/Sports Centre?   ....
Sue: No, I went there yesterday.
Mary: OK. Why/go/Smart Moves concert?   ....
Sue: No … the tickets are very expensive!
Mary: Well, have you got any ideas?
Sue: Let's/stay/home/watch TV   ....
Mary: That's not very exciting!
Sue: All right. Why/go/cinema?   ....
Mary: Good idea! I'll meet you there at 3 o'clock.

4 Would like

Here are some mixed-up *would like* questions.
Write each one correctly, then give a reply.

a drink/like/would/you/a/?
   Would you like a drink?   Yes, I would.

b match/to/would/watch/the/you/like/football/?
   ....

c you/eat/hamburger/would/a/to/like/?
   ....

d holiday/go/England/like/on/would/to/you/to/?
   ....

e like/you/meet/Britney/to/would/Spears/?
   ....

f very/to/like/be/would/rich/you/?
   ....

5 Future dreams
Think about your family, friends and pets, and say what you think each of them would like in the future.

a I would like ....
b My mother ....
c My ....
d My ....
e My ....
f My ....
g My ....
h My ....

6a Read this passage.

Carrots

Perhaps you will be surprised to learn that the orange carrots we know and love only came into European cooking recently. People ate purple and yellow carrots for more than 1,000 years before they grew the first modern orange carrot, probably in Holland, in the 18th century.

The carrot is a vegetable which is very good for our health. It contains many good things for our bodies. It has lots of Vitamin A, and also Vitamins B3, C and E, minerals and carotene. Everyone's mother tells you that 'carrots help you to see at night', but it is true in a way, because Vitamin A is important for the eyes.

People use carrots in many different ways. When you have washed and peeled them, you can eat them as they are, uncooked, like an apple. You can also cut them up and add them to salads. Young carrots are often very sweet, and make a much better snack at school than crisps.

People also cook carrots in water for about 10–15 minutes, and use them as a vegetable with other food like meat, fish and potatoes. They are good vegetables to put into soups and stews with other vegetables and meat. They also make an excellent soup on their own.

However, unlike most other vegetables, you can also use carrots to make cakes because of their sweetness. And they can be used to make a wonderful natural juice. So perhaps the carrot is the best vegetable you can get.

6b Answer these questions.

a What did carrots look like before the 18th century?

....

b Where was the first modern orange carrot probably grown?

....

c What part of our body are carrots especially good for? Why?

....

d What other good things do carrots contain?

....

e The article mentions four basic ways of using carrots. What are they?

....

f What is it about carrots that means they can be used in cakes?

....

6c Word meanings
Write definitions of the following words from the 'Carrots' passage.

a to peel:

....

....

b uncooked:

....

....

c salad:

....

....

d snack:

....

....

e stew:

....

....

f vitamin:

....

....

g health:

....

....

7 Summary writing

Write a summary of the passage about carrots on p. 56. There are five paragraphs. Write one sentence to summarise each paragraph.

Carrots: a summary

8 Guided writing

Write a passage about the food you like and don't like eating. Organise it so that you talk about similar things together (apples, bananas and pears together, then carrots, potatoes and cabbage together). Try to give a reason why you like and don't like the things you mention. Talk about taste, smell, and what they look like. Use your dictionary if you're not sure of the names of some of the foods. Write 100–150 words.

Food: what I like and don't like

9 Vocabulary
Write the correct word from the box in each space.
They are all new words from Unit 9.

| guests | ~~published~~ | poisonous | diet | fuel |
| coins | connect | poor | cure | flat |

a   John is a writer. Macmillan have just *published* his new book.
b   John hopes to get a lot of money from his book. Like many writers he is very ....
c   Mrs Jones went to see a new doctor. She hoped he could .... her.
d   Put this wire together with the other one, then when they .... the light will come on.
e   There are no hills or mountains in the east of England, so it is very ....
f   Don't eat the fruit on that tree! It's very .... !
g   I haven't got any banknotes left, just a few .... in my pocket.
h   Of course you can come to stay with us! We love having ....
i   You must eat lots of fruit and vegetables in order to have a good ....
j   Petrol for the car, wood for the fire, and food for us: they are all kinds of ....

10 Prepositions
Put one preposition in each space.

Sarah: Where did you get that coin (1) *from* ?
Peter: I found it (2) .... this old box. I've got lots (3) .... coins in my collection. I keep them (4) .... special books.
Sarah: What do you do (5) .... your coin collection?
Peter: I look (6) .... them, and try to get new ones. I sometimes get new coins when we go (7) .... holiday (8) .... different countries.
Sarah: I've got some coins (9) .... home. Would you like me to give them (10) .... you?
Peter: Yes, please. What kind (11) .... coins are they?
Sarah: There are some (12) .... Italy and France.

Unit 10

1 *Have to* **1**
Make sentences using the words below.

a home/I/make bed (+)/cook dinner (−)
At home I have to make my bed, but I don't have to cook the dinner.

b home/I/tidy room (+)/clean windows (−)
....

c school/we/wear jacket (+)/wear cap (−)
....

d park/you/walk path (+)/be quiet (−)
....

e home/she/wash car (+)/do shopping (−)
....

f concert/you/buy ticket (+)/sit numbered seat (−)
....

g school/he/go lessons (+)/play sports (−)
....

2a *Have to* **2: What sports?**
Look at the sports in the box, and the rules below. Decide which rule goes with each sport.

| tennis | football | ~~volleyball~~ | rugby | basketball | cricket |

a You have to hit the ball across the net with your hands.
There are six players in each team.
The sport is *volleyball* .

b You have to run with the ball in your hands and pass it.
There are 15 players in each team.
The sport is ....

c You have to hit the ball with a bat and try to score runs.
There are 11 players in each team.
The sport is ....

d You have to hit the ball across the net with a racket.
There are one or two people on each side of the net.
The sport is ....

e You have to run or walk bouncing the ball with your hands, and pass it. There are six players in each team.
The sport is ....

f You have to run and pass the ball with your feet.
There are 11 players in each team.
The sport is ....

60 sixty

2b Write about four more sports and ask your friend to guess what they are.

a You have to ....
....
The sport is ....

b You ....
....
The sport is ....

c You have to ....
....
The sport is ....

d You ....
....
The sport is ....

3 *Have to* 3: Questions and answers
Paul is talking to his grandfather. He is asking about what life was like when he was a boy. Make the answers positive if you see (+) and negative if you see (–).

1	Paul:	get up/early/?	*Did you get up early?*
	Grandfather:	+/get up/6	*Yes, we had to get up at 6 o'clock.*
2	Paul:	wash/hot water/?	....
	Grandfather:	–/wash/cold water	....
3	Paul:	eat/cooked breakfast/?	....
	Grandfather:	+/eat/bacon and eggs	....
4	Paul:	go/school/Monday to Friday/?	....
	Grandfather:	+/and/go/school/Saturday	....
5	Paul:	do/homework/evening/?	....
	Grandfather:	–/but/help/father's shop	....
6	Paul:	go/bed/early/?	....
	Grandfather:	+/be/bed/by 10 o'clock	....

4   *Have to* 4: Short answers
    Give short answers to these questions.

    a Do you have to go to school Monday to Friday?   *Yes, I do.*
    b Do you have to help your mother do the shopping?   ....
    c Do you have to wear a school uniform?   ....
    d Do you have to tidy your room every week?   ....
    e Do your parents have to go to work every day?   ....
    f Did your grandfather have to help his father work? ....
    g Do you have to practise an instrument every day?   ....
    h Do you have to help cook the dinner?   ....
    i Did your grandmother have to go to Sunday School? ....

5   Adverbs of manner 1
    Change the sentences with adjectives into sentences with adverbs.

    a He's a quiet worker.   *He works quietly.*
    b She's a healthy eater.   ....
    c They're slow runners.   ....
    d He's a good player.   ....
    e She's a careful cook.   ....
    f I'm a safe climber.   ....
    g He's a creative writer.   ....
    h He's a heavy sleeper.   ....
    i She's a beautiful dancer.   ....
    j He's a successful manager.   ....
    k They're skilful football players. ....

6   Adverbs of manner 2: Opposites
    Write sentences with the opposite adverbs in them.
    Make your adverbs from the adjectives in the box.

quiet	cold	bad	~~sad~~	slow	dangerous

    a He looked at her **happily**, she looked at him *sadly* .
    b He greeted her **warmly**, she greeted him ....
    c Mary played tennis **well**, Susan played tennis ....
    d John rode his bike **fast**, Peter rode his bike ....
    e The girls played their drums **noisily**, the boys played their guitars ....
    f Steve climbed the tree **carefully**, Mike climbed the tree ....

7 Vocabulary
Write the correct word from the box in each space.
They are all new words from Unit 10.

battery	opinion	complain	decision	panic
annually	bucket	delivers	competition	victory

a Every morning the milkman *delivers* three bottles of milk to our house.
b 'I'm very frightened!' 'Don't worry! There's no need to ....'
c I think it's a very good idea. What's your .... ?
d They hold the Olympic Games every four years, but they hold the European Championship ....
e 'What are you doing with that .... of water?' 'I'm going to clean the car.'
f I bought this radio yesterday but it doesn't work. I'm going to take it back to the shop and ....
g Every year the school has a .... to find the best painter in each class.
h Preston beat Birmingham 5–0. It was a really great .... !
i I don't know what to do. Shall I go or shall I stay? I must make a ....
j The lights on my bike don't work. I must need a new ....

8 Articles
Put an article (*a/an/the*) in each space, if necessary – leave a space if no article is necessary.

In (1) *the* village of Walton in (2) .... south of Rumboldia there is (3) .... strange tradition. On May 1st all (4) .... women meet in (5) .... village hall at (6) .... midnight. They all wear (7) .... old red dress and hat. They then go to every house in (8) .... village and knock at (9) .... door. (10) .... men who are inside then open (11) .... upstairs window, and throw (12) .... bucket of water over (13) .... women who are standing in (14) .... street. Nobody knows where this tradition came from, but it is very popular – especially with (15) .... men!

9 Read the passage, then answer the questions below.

Living Happily at Home

When children get past ten years old both they and their parents sometimes find it difficult to live together happily at home. This often happens because the children want to do different things from their parents, and because the parents still think their children are little babies.

Sometimes the children are right. They need to go out, meet their friends and learn how to live with people who are not part of the family. They need to do this to become successful adults.

Sometimes the parents are right. Children still need help, and there are many things about the world that they don't understand yet. Parents still have to teach their children what is good and bad, and how to live in the world outside the family.

So how can parents and children live happily at home? It is a matter of give and take on both sides. Children must not ask for too much. Parents must let their children move into the outside world.

The most important thing is to talk and listen to each other. Children have to explain to their parents what they want to do and why. Parents have to explain to their children what they can and can't do and why. Shouting, crying, hiding in your room, are not the way to live happily at home. Talking and listening openly is the answer.

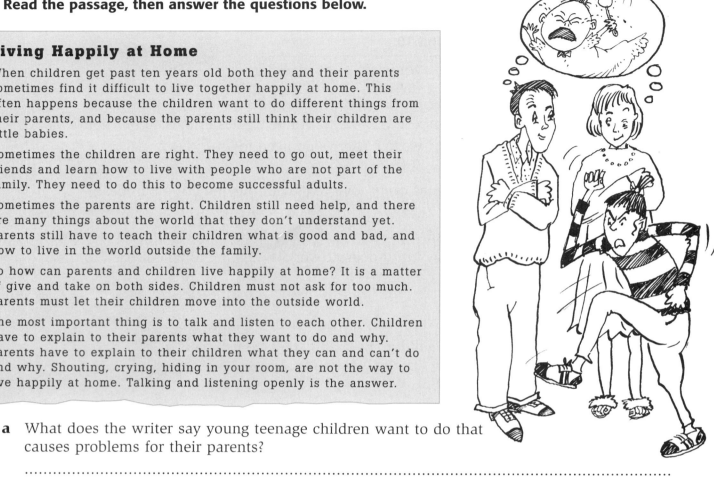

a What does the writer say young teenage children want to do that causes problems for their parents?

....
....

b Why does the writer say parents prevent their young teenage children from doing what they want?

....
....

c Who does the writer say is right: the children or the parents, and why?

....
....

d What does the writer say the children shouldn't do?

....
....

e What does the writer say the parents should do?

....
....

f What does the writer say is the answer to the problem?

....
....

10 Summary writing

Write a summary of the passage about living happily at home on p. 64. There are five paragraphs. Write one sentence to summarise the information in each paragraph.

Living Happily at Home: a summary
....
....
....
....
....
....
....

11 Guided writing

Write about life in your family. First describe your family, then write about what you like about each person, and what you don't like. Next discuss any problems you have at home, and try to say why you think they happen. Finish by saying how you think you can help to make your family life better. Write 120–150 words.

Life in my family
....
....
....
....
....
....
....
....
....
....
....
....
....

Stopover Two

1 Present perfect simple
Use the words in brackets to explain what has happened in each situation.

   a Susan is in class. She's looking for her homework in her bag.
(forget it) *Susan's forgotten her homework.*

   b Mum and Dad are coming back from the supermarket with lots of bags.
(buy food for the family) ....

   c John is coming out of his grandmother's house.
(visit his grandmother) ....

   d Paul is standing outside his front door looking worried.
(lose his key) ....

   e Mary is still standing outside the cinema.
(friend not come) ....

2 Present perfect simple or Past simple?
Choose the correct word.

   a I went to Paris last week but I *didn't visit/~~haven't visited~~* the Eiffel Tower.
   b I *liked/have liked* Paris very much.
   c We *haven't had/didn't have* any rain when we *have been/were* there.
   d *Have/Did* you ever *been/go* to Paris?
   e No, but I *have gone/went* to London when I *was/have been* a boy.
   f My mother *has taken/took* me there for my tenth birthday.

3 Choose the correct word in each sentence.

   a Where is *my/~~me~~/~~mine~~* bag? I left it here.
   b Peter forgot to take *he/him/his* homework to school this morning.
   c Janet told me that *she/her/hers* mother is ill again.
   d Mike and I are sitting at this desk – it's *ours/our/us*.
   e The Smith family aren't coming, so I've put *they/theirs/their* books on the shelf.
   f Have you got *your/you/yours*? I haven't got one.

4 *Have to* or *don't have to*?
Look at the list of things and write sentences about yourself,
saying what you *have to* and *don't have to* do.

   a make bed every day
   b do the family shopping
   c help in the kitchen
   d do my homework every school night
   e peel the potatoes
   f clean the family car

5 Vocabulary
Put the words in the box into the correct sentences.

| feel like doing | sightseeing | recycle | causes |
| rules | ~~can't stand~~ | peeled | celebrations |

a I don't want to sit by Steve. I *can't stand* him.
b It's a nice sunny day. What do you .... today?
c John and his brother have .... the vegetables for lunch.
d When I visit a new city I always like to go ....
e I don't understand how to play this game. Can you tell me the .... , please?
f Don't throw that bottle away. Take it to the place where they .... them.
g Every 4th July there are big .... in America for Independence Day.
h Do you know what .... most pollution in our city?

6 Shopping
Write what the people say in the spaces.

Good morning.

Good morning. Can (1) .... ?

Yes, please. I'd (2) .... to see some pullovers.

What (3) .... do you take?

I usually take a 28.

And how (4) .... do you want to pay?

Not more than £20.

This is a new style. What (5) .... do you want?

I prefer the green one.

Would (6) .... to try it on?

Yes, please.

Word List

Word List – Unit by Unit

Unit 1

advice /ad'vaɪs/
angle /'angəl /
astronomer /a'strɒnəmə(r)/
atmosphere /'atməsfɪə(r)/
autograph /ɔːtoʊgrɑːf/
be good at /bɪ gʊd at/
busy /'bɪzɪ/
candle /'kandəl/
cheer someone up /tʃɪə(r) sʌmwʌn ʌp/
companion /kəm'panjən/
could /kʊd/
cycle [v] /'saɪkəl/
definitely /'dɛfɪnətlɪ/
distant /'dɪstənt/
dizzy /'dɪzɪ/
face [v] /feɪs/
farm /fɑːm/
favourite /'feɪvərət/
find out /faɪnd aʊt/
fitness centre /'fɪtnɛs 'sɛntə(r)/
for fun /fɔː(r) fʌn/
galaxy /'galəksɪ/
giant [adj] /dʒaɪənt/
give someone advice /gɪv sʌmwʌn ad'vaɪs/
hurt /hɜːt/
information /ɪnfə'meɪʃən/
information technology
   /ɪnfə'meɪʃən tɛk'nɒlədʒɪ/
journey /'dʒɜːnɪ/
keep a secret /kiːp ə 'sɪkrət/
laugh at /lɑːf at/
lens /lɛnz/
manager /'manɪdʒə(r)/
mirror /'mɪrə(r)/
miss /mɪs/
Moon /muːn/
object /əb'dʒɛkt/
observatory /əb'zɜːvətərɪ/
perform /pə'fɔːm/
play [n] /pleɪ/
raincoat /reɪnkoʊt/

receive /rɪ'siːv/
recording studio /rɪ'kɔːdɪŋ 'stʃuːdɪoʊ/
satisfied /'satɪsfaɪd/
scientist /'saɪəntɪst/
send /sɛnd/
share [v] /ʃɛə(r)/
show [n] /ʃoʊ/
signal /'sɪgnəl/
sky /skaɪ/
spin [v] /spɪn/
star /stɑː/
telescope /'tɛlɪskoʊp/
tilt /tɪlt/
universe /'juːnɪvɜːs/
university /juːnɪ'vɜːsɪtɪ/
waste of time /weɪst əv taɪm/

Unit 2

arrangement /ə'reɪndʒmənt/
attempt [n] /ə'tɛmt/
audience /'ɔːdɪəns/
ballpoint /'bɔːlpɔɪnt/
cancel /'kansəl/
castaway /'kɑːstəweɪ/
cave /keɪv/
expect /ɪk'spɛkt/
fall over /fɔːl 'oʊvə(r)/
find the way /faɪnd θə weɪ/
get by /gɛt baɪ/
goat /goʊt/
hut /hʌt/
invention /ɪn'vɛnʃən/
lecture [n] /'lɛktʃə(r)/
lend a hand /lɛnd ə hand/
length /lɛŋθ/
look after /lʊk 'ɑːftə(r)/
look forward to /lʊk 'fɔːwəd tuː/
message /'mɛsɪdʒ/
on stage /ɒn steɪdʒ/
passing /pɑːsɪŋ/
performance /pə'fɔːməns/
quick /kwɪk/
remain /rɪ'meɪn/
rescue /'rɛskjuː/
shellfish /ʃɛlfɪʃ/

Word List

sink /sɪnk/
stage /steɪdʒ/
stream /striːm/
talented /taləntəd/
tool /tuːl/
turn out /tɜːn aʊt/
unfortunately /ʌnˈfɔːtʃənətlɪ/
uninhabited /ʌnɪnˈhabɪtəd/
unsafe /ʌnseɪf/
vegetable /ˈvedʒtəbəl/
voyage /ˈvɔɪɪdʒ/

Unit 3

approach /əˈproʊtʃ/
armed /ɑːmd/
arrest /əˈrɛst/
billion /ˈbɪlɪən/
bin /bɪn/
chimpanzee /tʃɪmpanˈziː/
copy [n] /ˈkɒpɪ/
crash [v] /kraʃ/
diamond /ˈdaɪəmənd/
donate /doʊˈneɪt/
doughnut /ˈdoʊnʌt/
dress as /drɛs az/
drought /draʊt/
eventually /ɪˈventʃʊelɪ/
exhibition /ɛksɪˈbɪʃən/
fire engine /faɪə(r) ˈɛndʒɪn/
getaway car /ɡɛtəweɪ kɑː/
make a mess /meɪk ə mɛs/
mask /mɑːsk/
milk shake /mɪlk ʃeɪk/
paw /pɔː/
power boat /ˈpaʊə(r) boʊt/
queue [v] /kjuː/
raid [n] /reɪd/
raise money /reɪz ˈmʌnɪ/
servant /ˈsɛːvənt/
slip /slɪp/
starve /stɑːv/
surrender /səˈrɛndə(r)/
sweep /swiːp/
upset /ʌpˈsɛt/
view [n] /vjuː/

Unit 4

active /ˈaktɪv/
ancestor /ˈansəstə(r)/
as different as chalk and cheese /az ˈdɪfərənt
    az tʃɔːk and tʃːz/
at heart /at hɑːt/
axe /aks/
brain /breɪn/
brighten up /braɪtən ʌp/
cheap /tʃiːp/
climate /ˈklaɪmət/
comfortable /ˈkʌmfətəbəl/
creative /krɪˈeɪtɪv/
creature /ˈkriːtʃə(r)/
deep /diːp/
dry /draɪ/
eldest /ˈɛldɪst/
forest /ˈfɒrəst/
frightening /fraɪtənɪŋ/
healthy /ˈhɛlθɪ/
heavy /ˈhɛvɪ/
hunt [v] /hʌnt/
light /laɪt/
lively /ˈlaɪvlɪ/
lovely /ˈlʌvlɪ/
lucky /ˈlʌkɪ/
mobile phone /ˈmoʊbaɪl foʊn/
previous /ˈpriːvɪəs/
rodent /ˈroʊdənt/
sad /sad/
size /saɪz/
skilful /ˈskɪlfəl/
sociable /ˈsoʊʃəbəl/
take the place of /teɪk ðə pleɪs əv/
tasty /ˈteɪstɪ/
try something on /traɪ sʌmθɪŋ ɒn/
waterfall /ˈwɔːtə(r)fɔːl/
weigh /weɪ/

Unit 5

appearance /əˈpɪərəns/
bacon /ˈbeɪkən/
borrow /ˈbɒroʊ/
common /ˈkɒmən/

sixty nine 69

crowded /ˈkraʊdəd/
factory /ˈfaktərɪ/
fall ill /fɔːl ɪl/
frame /freɪm/
government /ˈgʌvəmənt/
imaginary /ɪˈmadʒɪnərɪ/
invent /ɪnˈvɛnt/
lawn /lɔːn/
leaflet /ˈliːflət/
look like /lʊk laɪk/
married /ˈmarɪd/
mechanical /məˈkanɪkəl/
packed lunch /pakd lʌntʃ/
polluted /pəˈluːtəd/
produce /prəˈdʒuːs/
recognise /ˈrɛkəgnaɪz/
replace /rɪˈpleɪs/
resolution /rɛzəˈluːʃən/
rule [v] /ruːl/
skin /skɪn/
suit [n] /suːt/
take over /teɪk ˈoʊvə(r)/
tidy [v] /ˈtaɪdɪ/
together /təˈgɛðə(r)/
wash up /wɒʃ ʌp/

Unit 6

acid rain /ˈasɪd reɪn/
amount /əˈmaʊnt/
capital /ˈkapɪtəl/
cause [n] /kɔːz/
cause [v] /kɔːz/
central heating /ˈsɛntrəl hiːtɪŋ/
close up /kloʊs ʌp/
cut down /kʌt daʊn/
depend on /dɪˈpɛnd ɒn/
disappear /dɪsəˈpɪə(r)/
do [our] bit /duː [aʊə(r)] bɪt/
energy /ˈɛnədʒɪ/
fridge /frɪdʒ/
gas /gas/
key /kiː/
level /ˈlɛvəl/
lion carton /ˈlaɪən ˈkaːtən/
lose /luːz/

melt /mɛlt/
nowadays /ˈnaʊədeɪz/
ocean /ˈoʊʃən/
ordinary /ˈɔːdɪnərɪ/
petrol /ˈpɛtrəl/
plant [v] /plaːnt/
pollution /pəˈluːʃən/
recycle /rɪsaɪkəl/
sauce /sɔːs/
tap /tap/
temperature /ˈtɛmpərətʃə(r)/
toy /tɔɪ/
tractor /ˈtraktə(r)/
turn down /tɜːn daʊn/
turn off /tɜːn ɒf/
wallet /ˈwɒlɪt/
waste [v] /weɪst/
wild flower /waɪld flaʊə(r)/
wildlife park /ˈwaɪldlaɪf paːk/

Unit 7

adult /ˈadʌlt/
attached to /əˈtatʃt tuː/
aware /əˈwɛə(r)/
blindfold /ˈblaɪndfoʊld/
board game /bɔːd geɪm/
calculator /ˈkalkjuleɪtə(r)/
catch /katʃ/
cause a disturbance /ˈkɔːz ə dɪˈstɜːbəns/
commit a foul /kəˈmɪt ə faʊl/
completely /kəmˈpliːtlɪ/
concentrate /ˈkɒnsəntreɪt/
corner /ˈkɔːnə(r)/
diameter /daɪˈamɪtə(r)/
diving board /ˈdaɪvɪŋ bɔːd/
duty /ˈdʒuːtɪ/
electrical equipment /ɪˈlɛktrɪkəl ɪˈkwɪpmənt/
entry /ˈɛntrɪ/
fall in /fɔːl ɪn/
forearm /ˈfɔːraːm/
free /friː/
hang /haŋ/
hop /hɒp/
huge /hjuːdʒ/
include /ɪnˈkluːd/

label /ˈleɪbəl/
litter /ˈlɪtə(r)/
loads of /ˈloʊds əv/
luggage /ˈlʌɡɪdʒ/
make someone do something /meɪk sʌmwʌn duː sʌmθɪŋ/
make sure /meɪk ʃʊə(r)/
make-up /meɪkʌp/
masses of /masəs əv/
membership /ˈmɛmbərʃɪp/
pile /paɪl/
plenty /ˈplɛntɪ/
pole /poʊl/
present /ˈprɛzənt/
proper /ˈprɒpə(r)/
receipt /rɪˈsiːt/
sale [n] /seɪl/
score /skɔː/
search /sɜːtʃ/
serve /sɜːv/
shower gel /ˈʃaʊə(r) dʒɛl/
skirt /skɜːt/
square /skwɛə(r)/
stay up /steɪ ʌp/
strike /straɪk/
take away /teɪk əˈweɪ/
tie /taɪ/
time restriction /taɪm rɪˈstrɪkʃən/
towel /ˈtaʊəl/
waterproof /ˈwɔːtə(r)pruːf/
wind [v] /waɪnd/

Unit 8

a bit strange /ˈə bɪt streɪndʒ/
angry /ˈaŋɡrɪ/
bridge /brɪdʒ/
building /bɪldɪŋ/
can't stand /kɑːnt ˈstand/
colony /ˈkɒlənɪ/
cry /kraɪ/
damage /ˈdamɪdʒ/
destroy /dɪˈstrɔɪ/
discovery /dɪsˈkʌvərɪ/
dish /dɪʃ/
earthquake /ˈɜːəkweɪk/
event /ɪˈvɛnt/

exchange student /ɪksˈtʃeɪndʒ ˈstjuːdənt/
expert /ˈɛkspɜːt/
feel fine /fiːl faɪn/
fox /fɒks/
freeze /friːz/
fur /fɜː(r)/
gold /ɡoʊld/
improve /ɪmˈpruːv/
industry /ˈɪndəstrɪ/
lie /laɪ/
local /ˈloʊkəl/
made of /meɪd ɒv/
make friends /meɪk frɛnds/
mention /ˈmɛnʃən/
motorway /ˈmoʊtə(r)weɪ/
nervous /ˈnɜːvəs/
oil /ɔɪl/
polar bear /ˈpoʊlə(r) bɛə(r)/
population /pɒpjʊˈleɪʃən/
round the corner /raʊnd θə ˈkɔːnə(r)/
seal /siːl/
sea otter /siː ˈɒtə(r)/
serious /ˈsɪərɪəs/
settle in /ˈsɛtəl ɪn/
shy /ʃaɪ/
sightseeing /saɪtsiɪŋ/
snowmobile /ˈsnoʊməbiːl/
spill /spɪl/
suffer from /ˈsʌfə(r) frɒm/
teen band /tiːn band/
traditional /trəˈdɪʃənəl/
way of life /weɪ əv laɪf/
whale /weɪl/
zoo /zuː/

Unit 9

attachment /əˈtatʃmənt/
back /bak/
coin /kɔɪn/
connect /kəˈnɛkt/
cure /kjʊə(r)/
diet /ˈdaɪət/
digital clock /ˈdɪdʒɪtəl klɒk/
dig up /dɪɡ ʌp/
feel like /fiːl laɪk/
flat /flat/

flour /flaʊə(r)/
food value /fuːd 'valjuː/
fuel /fjʊəl/
galvanised /galvənaɪzd/
gardener /'gɑːdənə(r)/
go shopping /goʊ ʃɒpɪŋ/
grow /groʊ/
guest /gɛst/
health /hɛlθ/
illness /ɪlnəs/
insulated wire /'ɪnsjʊleɪtəd waɪə/
invader /ɪn'veɪdə(r)/
invite /ɪn'vaɪt/
live on /lɪv ɒn/
millionaire /mɪljə'nɛə(r)/
nail /neɪl/
native [adj] /'neɪtɪv/
on [one's] way /ɒn [wʌns] weɪ/
order /'ɔːdə(r)/
peel [v] /piːl/
poisonous /pɔɪzənəs/
politician /pɒlɪ'tɪʃən/
poor /pɔː(r)/
publish /'pʌblɪʃ/
root /ruːt/
silver /'sɪlvə(r)/
tired /taɪə(r)d/
vitamin /'vɪtəmɪn/
wrap /rap/

Unit 10

alternative /ɒl'tɜːnətɪv/
amplifier /'amplɪfaɪə(r)/
annoying /ə'nɔɪɪŋ/
annually /anjʊəlɪ/
as a team /az ə tiːm/
battery /'batərɪ/
boarding school /bɔːdɪŋ skuːl/
bucket /'bʌkɪt/
button /'bʌtən/
celebration /'sɛlə'breɪʃən/
chef /ʃɛf/
coincide /koʊɪn'saɪd/
come out /kʌm aʊt/
competition /kɒmpə'tɪʃən/
complain /kəm'pleɪn/

decision /dɪ'sɪʒən/
deliver /dɪ'lɪvə(r)/
double [v] /'dʌbəl/
embarrassed /ɪm'barəst/
fight [n] /faɪt/
fireworks /faɪə(r)wɜːks/
fit [adj] /fɪt/
friend and foe /frɛnd and foʊ/
frying pan /fraɪɪŋ pan/
get ready /gɛt 'rɛdɪ/
head [v] /hɛd/
join in /dʒɔɪn ɪn/
keep quiet /kiːp kwaɪət/
lorry /'lɒrɪ/
make a bed /meɪk ə bɛd/
make notes /meɪk noʊts/
martial arts /mɑːʃəl ɑːts/
messy /'mɛsɪ/
normal /'nɔməl/
on your own /ɒn jɔː(r) oʊn/
on your side /ɒn jɔː(r) saɪd/
opinion /ə'pɪnjən/
out [not at home] /aʊt/
pancake /pankeɪk/
panic [v] /'panɪk/
parade /pə'reɪd/
passer-by /pɑːsə(r)baɪ/
patron saint /peɪtrən seɪnt/
politely /pə'laɪtlɪ/
prepare for /prɪ'pɛə(r) fɔː(r)/
press /prɛs/
put up with /pʊt ʌp wɪð/
religious /rɪ'lɪdʒəs/
rules /ruːls/
seriously /'sɪərɪəslɪ/
shake-up /ʃeɪkʌp/
short of /ʃɔːt əv/
solution /sə'luːʃən/
squashed /skwɒʃd/
stage [v] /steɪdʒ/
stormy /'stɔːmɪ/
successful /sək'sɛsfəl/
tomato /tə'mɑːtoʊ/
underline /'ʌndə(r)laɪn/
victory /'vɪktərɪ/
vision /'vɪʒən/
wind up /waɪnd ʌp/